Short Walks
around
Loch Lomond
and
The Trossachs

Guide to 20 easy walks of 3 hours or less

Published by Collins
An imprint of HarperCollins Publishers
Westerhill Road
Bishopbriggs
Glasgow G64 2QT

www.harpercollins.co.uk

First edition 2012

Copyright © HarperCollins Publishers Ltd 2012

Original text © Gilbert Summers

Collins © is a registered trademark of
HarperCollins Publishers Limited

Mapping on the inner front cover and all
walking planning maps generated from
Collins Bartholomew digital databases

This product uses map data licensed from
Ordnance Survey ® with the permission of the
Controller of Her Majesty's Stationery Office.
© Crown copyright. Licence number 399302

Printed in China

ISBN 978 0 00 746454 8

email: roadcheck@harpercollins.co.uk

Follow us on twitter @CollinsMaps

Contents

▶ Short walks

Introduction

Loch Lomond

Walking around Loch Lomond and The Trossachs

This is an area of contrast and the choice of walks reflects this. Not all of them are Highland as two of the routes are on or near the Ochils close to Stirling. They are included, not only as a foretaste of more heathery hills further west, but as interesting viewpoints in themselves.

The Callander area to the north-east provides another focal point. Many visitors will be surprised to find how easy it is to escape the busy tourist streets. The northern borders of the area covered are reached on a walk making use of a disused railway in Glen Ogle while more centrally, in addition to forestry roads and tracks, advantage has been taken of the surfaced road around Loch Katrine. The Trossachs are explored from many angles, wherever access permits.

Loch Lomond, with its rugged and steeper terrain in the north and tendency to sprout 'private' notices in the south, has been covered partly by dipping into the West Highland Way, Scotland's first long-distance footpath. In this rugged area in particular, the walks have been chosen with care, bearing in mind the relatively inexperienced walker. Equally, they have been chosen to make the most of Loch Lomond's famed beauty. Ben Lomond looms impressively on its eastern shore and secret places still survive surprisingly close to the rush of traffic along the A82.

Walking is a pastime which can fulfil the needs of everyone. You can adapt it to suit your own preferences and it is one of the healthiest of activities. This guide is for those who just want to walk a few miles. It really doesn't take long to find yourself in some lovely countryside. All the walks should easily be completed in under three hours. Walking can be anything from an individual pastime to a family stroll, or maybe a group of friends enjoying the fresh air and open spaces of our countryside. There is no need for walking to be competitive and, to get the most from a walk, it shouldn't be regarded simply as a means of covering a given distance in the shortest possible time.

Geology and Landscape

The Highland Boundary Fault lies across the area covered in this book. It will be noticeable on many of the walks that the views give Highland and lowland contrasts. The fault line that separates the Highlands from the Scottish Midland Valley runs through Loch Lomond, Balmaha, the Menteith Hills, Loch Venachar and on, north-eastwards. Below it, the immediate lowlands are mainly sandstone on which very recent glacial action has dumped other rocks and gravels, though the Ochils are built of ancient lavas, also present less significantly in the Menteith Hills. Northwards, complicated bands of conglomerate, slates, and schistose grits are not easily comprehended by the amateur eye. As a simplification, it is enough to remember that the northern rock types are harder and more resistant to weathering than the sandstones immediately to the south. These northern Dalradian rocks (named after Dalradia, the first Scottish kingdom) are variable in appearance, some still showing their gritty origins on the floors of ancient seas, while others through heat and pressure have 'metamorphosed'. Probably the commonest are the schists, grey in appearance, sometimes streaked with parallel bands of other minerals.

The present-day landscape owes much to the differing degrees of hardness of these rocks, with the most resistant schistose grits forming the conspicuous bulk of Ben Lomond and Ben Ledi. After these ancient rock movements, much more recent Ice Ages (the last as recent as 10,000 years ago) stripped and plucked at the rough shapes, deepening and scouring valleys, dumping and damming to create major lochs such as Loch Lomond. Now, modern man has wrought other basic landscape changes. Electric power and water supply needs have resulted in the tampering with Lochs Sloy, Venachar, Katrine, Arklet, Drunkie and a few other waters in the vicinity.

Loch Katrine in the Trossachs

History

Once, most of the area north of the Highland Boundary Fault was truly 'Highland' in the sense that its Celtic population lived by an economy adapted to a mountainous terrain. The clan system meant that families in any one community owed allegiance to the local chief. Some of the families would hold land as 'tacksmen' or relatives of the chief, others would pay rent in turn to these tacksmen. This system had evolved by about the mid 13th century. There was both a physical mountain barrier and a language separating these tribal units from the lowlands to the south.

Just over the barrier, the feudal barons were powerful. For example, Doune Castle, near Callander, was the centre of a large block of territory, held in the name of the Dukes of Albany. In those very distant times, the Earls of Lennox held sway over the south end of Loch Lomond from an earlier Balloch Castle. The Menteith Grahams were powerful in the area between. There is no space here to pursue the complexities of the area's history, but it must be said that the lowland landowners were not always successful in keeping the Highland clansmen from raiding southwards. Besides, for many of them, there were political careers to pursue elsewhere. News from their own tenants that yet another score of cattle had vanished into the mountains was extremely inconvenient. Things became so bad along the Highland/lowland border that, on occasion, the Scottish kings were even asked to intervene. From Edinburgh's Holyrood House in 1585 an edict was issued, summoning the local landowners to Stirling: 'The King and his council, being informed that his good and peaceable subjects inhabiting the countries of Lennox, Menteith, Stirlingshire and Strathearn are heavily oppressed by reif, stouth and sorning and other crimes daily and nightly'. The three unfamiliar words mean plundering, theft and squatting - the last mentioned also involved using weapons to fend off any attempt to collect rent.

At one time 'sorning' was a particular problem in Balquhidder Glen, though by the 17th century the glen was nominally controlled by the Murray family with headquarters in far away Blair Castle. Unquestionably, north of the Highland line, life was hard – little wonder that black cattle were lifted with regularity from the lowland fields. They provided a kind of 'welfare state' on the hoof – a handy currency to see a family through a bad winter. One clansman who appreciated this from an early age was a certain Rob Roy MacGregor.

Rob Roy MacGregor

The Kirkton Glen walk (Walk 1) starts from Rob Roy's graveside, while the Loch Katrineside excursion (Walk 13) is to the scene of his childhood. He was born in Glen Gyle of the Clan Gregor, who at the time were being tolerated by a monarchy which had actually outlawed the entire clan earlier in the century, for the kind of reasons mentioned in the previous section. His career cannot be separated from the time in which he lived. The reign of the Stuart monarchy was ending. Born in 1671, as a teenager, Rob would hear of the succession of the House of Hanover,

Grave of Rob Roy MacGregor

yet he remained a Jacobite (a supporter of the Stuart claimants) all his life, no doubt acquiring these sympathies from an early age through his own father who served in the army of the Stuart King Charles II.

He is remembered today, not just through the romantic portrait painted by Sir Walter Scott in his novel *Rob Roy*, but partly because in those lawless times, he, in effect, challenged the government, which in spite of all the resources of the 'British' army, was unable to bring him in. Sir Walter certainly saw him as the symbol of a Highland way of life, proud and independent, that was to vanish utterly with the advance of lowland 'civilisation' and the final dismantling of the clan system after Culloden in 1746.

The 'real' Rob Roy rose to notoriety through his dealings in the cattle trade, as a semi-legitimate drover, dealer and opportunist with one eye on the lowland herds. Superb swordsmanship, survival skills and hill craft enabled him to defend property on the hoof, both his own and his 'clients'. This was noticed by the very powerful Duke of Montrose, who owned substantial grounds around Loch Lomond (and was a Hanoverian, too). A deal was struck. Rob was to use the Duke's money to buy and fatten cattle, with profits shared. However, the money disappeared while in the hands of one of Rob's own trusted drovers. Rather than give Rob time to repay the funds and with the most questionable of motives (Rob owned some lands on the east bank of Loch Lomond – now crossed by the West Highland Way), the Duke promptly declared him an outlaw and seized his house and lands. Thus, in 1712, a desperate phase of the MacGregor's life began.

He was, after all, 'hot property' – a man of skill and craft in an unstable political climate. He was within the sphere of operations of not only Montrose, but also another baron of high office - the Duke of Argyll, who was to command the government forces against the rebel Jacobites at Sheriffmuir three years later. (You are near the battle site on the Dumyat walk.) Rob played a large part in this rebellion. Montrose wanted him to implicate Argyll in a Jacobite plot, with the return of Rob's lands if he bore false witness against Argyll, Montrose's political opponent.

He refused and instead redoubled his raiding on Montrose lands. He was captured on more than one occasion, but always managed to escape. Another major landowner, the Duke of Atholl, even managed to capture him through treachery, but Rob escaped again and made his way to Balquhidder. A network of sympathisers and intelligence gatherers, plus supreme survival skills, meant that Rob, even after playing a part in the rebellion at Glenshiel in 1719, could gradually re-emerge to pursue the life of a cattle dealer, with a little semi-legitimate protectionism, in Balquhidder. There was eventually a reconciliation between all parties and Rob was to die peacefully in 1734. In his years of hardship as a fugitive, he paid the price for his refusal to become a part of lowland power squabbles, while remaining true to the Jacobite cause and evading all attempts to be brought to lowland justice.

Loch Lomond and the Trossachs National Park

Loch Lomond and The Trossachs National Park was the first of two national parks which were established by the Scottish Parliament in 2002, with the second national park being the Cairngorms. The national park is centred on Loch Lomond and includes several ranges of hills, with the Trossachs being the most famous.

It is the fourth largest national park in the British Isles and covers an area of 720 square miles (1865 sq km) with a boundary measuring approximately 220 miles (350km) in length. The national park includes 21 Munros (including Ben Lomond), 20 Corbetts, two forest parks (Queen Elizabeth and Argyll) and 57 designated special nature conservation sites.

For further information on the Park, and for a greater understanding of the area, visit the National Park visitor centre at the southern end of Loch Lomond. The centre is called Loch Lomond Shores and includes a visitor information centre, as well as an aquarium, shops and restaurants.

View from summit of Ben Lomond

Walking tips & guidance

Safety

As with all other outdoor activities, walking is safe provided a few simple common sense rules are followed:

- Make sure you are fit enough to complete the walk;

- Always try to let others know where you intend going, especially if you are walking alone;

- Be clothed adequately for the weather and always wear suitable footwear;

- Always allow plenty of time for the walk, especially if it is longer or harder than you have done before;

- Whatever the distance you plan to walk, always allow plenty of daylight hours unless you are absolutely certain of the route;

- If mist or bad weather come on unexpectedly, do not panic but instead try to remember the last certain feature which you have passed (road, farm, wood, etc.). Then work out your route from that point on the map but be sure of your route before continuing;

- Do not dislodge stones on the high edges: there may be climbers or other walkers on the lower crags and slopes;

- Unfortunately, accidents can happen even on the easiest of walks. If this should be the case and you need the help of others, make sure that the injured person is safe in a place where no further injury is likely to occur. For example, the injured person should not be left on a steep hillside or in danger from falling rocks. If you have a mobile phone and there is a signal, call for assistance. If, however, you are unable to contact help by mobile and you cannot leave anyone with the injured person, and even if they are conscious, try to leave a written note explaining their injuries and whatever you have done in the way of first aid treatment. Make sure you know exactly where you left them and then go to find assistance. Make your way to a telephone, dial 999 and ask for the police or mountain rescue. Unless the accident has happened within easy access of a road, it is the responsibility of the police to arrange evacuation. Always give accurate directions on how to find the casualty and, if possible, give an indication of the injuries involved;

- When walking in open country, learn to keep an eye on the immediate foreground while you admire the scenery or plan the route ahead. This may sound difficult but will enhance your walking experience;

- It's best to walk at a steady pace, always on the flat of the feet as this is less tiring. Try not to walk directly up or downhill. A zigzag route is a more comfortable way of negotiating a slope. Running directly downhill is a major cause of erosion on popular hillsides;

- When walking along a country road, walk on the right, facing the traffic. The exception to this rule is, when approaching a blind bend, the walker should cross over to the left and so have a clear view and also be seen in both directions;

- Finally, always park your car where it will not cause inconvenience to other road users or prevent a farmer from gaining access to his fields. Take any valuables with you or lock them out of sight in the car.

Equipment

Equipment, including clothing, footwear and rucksacks, is essentially a personal thing and depends on several factors, such as the type of activity planned, the time of year, and weather likely to be encountered.

All too often, a novice walker will spend money on a fashionable jacket but will skimp when it comes to buying footwear or a comfortable rucksack. Blistered and tired feet quickly remove all enjoyment from even the most exciting walk and a poorly balanced rucksack will soon feel as though you are carrying a ton of bricks. Well designed equipment is not only more comfortable but, being better made, it is longer lasting.

Clothing should be adequate for the day. In summer, remember to protect your head and neck, which are particularly vulnerable in a strong sun and use sun screen. Wear light woollen socks and lightweight boots or strong shoes. A spare pullover and waterproofs carried in the rucksack should, however, always be there in case you need them.

A small word about a small problem – the infamous Highland Midge. Some visitors may have mused that there must have been a conspiracy of silence over this less-than-endearing feature of life in the Highlands. Certainly, few glossy tourism brochures give it any space, but it is fair to point out that in still conditions, on mild days near bodies of water in particular, the uniformly sadistic members of the Ceratopogonidae family may make their presence felt. Long-sleeved shirts are therefore preferable, and you are advised to carry a repellent, which usually needs frequent re-application. Different people react in differing degrees to their bites, but the attentions of any of the twenty-nine different blood-sucking species can be a little annoying.

Winter wear is a much more serious affair. Remember that once the body starts to lose heat, it becomes much less efficient. Jeans are particularly unsuitable for winter wear and can sometimes even be downright dangerous.

Waterproof clothing is an area where it pays to buy the best you can afford. Make sure that the jacket is loose-fitting, windproof and has a generous hood. Waterproof overtrousers will not only offer complete protection in the rain but they are also windproof. Do not be misled by flimsy nylon 'showerproof' items. Remember, too, that garments made from rubberised or plastic material are heavy to carry and wear and they trap body condensation. Your rucksack should have wide, padded carrying straps for comfort.

It is important to wear boots that fit well or shoes with a good moulded sole – blisters can ruin any walk! Woollen socks are much more comfortable than any other fibre. Your clothes should be comfortable and not likely to catch on twigs and bushes.

It is important to carry a compass, preferably one of the 'Silva' type as well as this guide. A smaller scale map covering a wider area can add to the enjoyment of a walk. Binoculars are not essential but are very useful for spotting distant stiles and give added interest to viewpoints and wildlife. Although none of the walks in this guide venture too far from civilisation, on a hot day even the shortest of walks can lead to dehydration so a bottle of water is advisable.

Finally, a small first aid kit is an invaluable help in coping with cuts and other small injuries.

Enjoy Scotland's outdoors responsibly
Know the code before you go

Everyone has the right to be on most land and inland water providing they act responsibly. Your access rights and responsibilities are explained fully in the Scottish Outdoor Access Code.

Whether you're in the outdoors or managing the outdoors, the key things are to:

- Take responsibility for your own actions;

- Respect the interests of other people;

- Care for the environment.

Visit outdooraccess-scotland.com or contact your local Scottish Natural Heritage office for further information.

Responsible access can be enjoyed over most of Scotland including:
- Urban parks;
- Hills and woods;
- Most grass fields and field margins;
- Beaches;
- Lochs, rivers and canals.

Access rights cover many activities including:
- Informal pastimes such as walking, camping, picnicking and sightseeing;
- Active pursuits including cycling, mountaineering, canoeing and horse riding;
- Dog walking, provided your dog is under proper control;
- Taking part in recreational and educational trips;
- Simply going from one place to another.

Places and activities not covered include:
- Buildings and their immediate surroundings;
- Houses and their gardens;
- Most land where crops are growing;
- Motorised activities (unless for disabled access);
- Hunting, shooting and fishing.

Getting out and about
Access Rights
The Land Reform (Scotland) Act 2003 gives you some of the best access rights in the world. You have the right to be on most land and inland water for recreation, education and going from place to place, providing you act responsibly. Your access rights and responsibilities are explained in the Scottish Outdoor Access Code.

Respect the interests of others
Respect the needs of other people enjoying or working in the outdoors and follow any reasonable advice from land managers. Respect people's privacy and peace of mind. Avoid causing alarm to people, especially at night, by keeping a reasonable distance from houses and gardens or by using paths or tracks.

West Highland Way sign

Care for the environment
Our environment contributes greatly to everyone's health and quality of life so treat it with care. Take your rubbish home and consider picking up other litter as well. Don't disturb or damage wildlife or historic places. Keep your dog on a short lead or under close control where needed.

Take responsibility for your own actions
The outdoors is a great place to enjoy but it's also a working environment and natural hazards exist. Make sure you are aware of this, take care of yourself and others with you, including your dog.

Heading for the hills
Most red stag stalking takes place between July and October, although this does vary. Follow all advice from the land manager or visit outdooraccess-scotland.com for advice on where deer management, stalking and shooting may be taking place.

Ground nesting birds
Reduce the chance of your dog disturbing birds during the nesting season (usually from April to July) by keeping your dog on a short lead or under close control in areas such as moorland, loch and sea shores, woods and grasslands.

In the woods

Fire warning
Never light fires during dry periods in woodlands or on peaty ground. Never cut down or damage trees. Use a stove carefully and leave no trace of any camp fire.

In the woods
Keep away from log piles and machinery. Pay attention to signs and follow any advice from the forester or land manager.

On and by the water

Sharing a path
Let people know you are coming so you do not alarm them. You might need to slow down, stop or stand aside to allow others to pass. Try to call out a friendly warning if you approach a horse and rider from behind.

Camping out
Leave no trace of your campsite. If public toilets aren't available, carry a trowel and bury your own waste and urinate well away from open water, rivers and burns.

Going paddling
Keep an eye out for anglers. If you see someone fishing, think about how you can best pass them with the least disturbance.

On the farm

Farmyards
Access rights do not usually apply to farmyards. However, if a right of way or core path goes through a farmyard, you can follow this at any time.

Gates
Use a gate or stile where one has been provided. Do not climb over walls or hedges unless there is no alternative. Leave gates as you find them – even if they are open. If you need to climb a gate, climb it at the hinge end.

Fields of farm animals or growing crops
Keep to unsown ground, field edges or paths. Do not take your dog into

fields containing growing crops, calves, lambs, or other young animals. Never let your dog worry or attack farm animals.

Safety around cattle
Keep a safe distance from cattle. If they act aggressively, take the shortest safest route out of the field. If you have a dog with you, let go of its lead and let it find its own way to safety.

From outdooraccess-scotland.com

Map reading

Some people find map reading so easy that they can open a map and immediately relate it to the area of countryside in which they are standing. To others, a map is as unintelligible as ancient Greek! A map is an accurate but flat picture of the three-dimensional features of the countryside. Features such as roads, streams, woodland and buildings are relatively easy to identify, either from their shape or position. Heights, on the other hand, can be difficult to interpret from the single dimension of a map. The Ordnance Survey 1:25,000 mapping used in this guide shows the contours at 5 metre intervals. Summits and spot heights are also shown.

The best way to estimate the angle of a slope, as shown on any map, is to remember that if the contour lines come close together then the slope is steep – the closer together the contours the steeper the slope.

Learn the symbols for features shown on the map and, when starting out on a walk, line up the map with one or more features, which are recognisable both from the map and on the ground. In this way, the map will be correctly positioned relative to the terrain. It should then only be necessary to look from the map towards the footpath or objective of your walk and then make for it! This process is also useful for determining your position at any time during the walk.

Let's take the skill of map reading one stage further: sometimes there are no easily recognisable features nearby: there may be the odd clump of trees and a building or two but none of them can be related exactly to the map. This is a frequent occurrence but there is a simple answer to the problem and this is where the use of a compass comes in. Simply place the map on the ground, or other flat surface, with the compass held gently above the map. Turn the map until the edge is parallel to the line of the compass needle, which should point to the top of the map. Lay the compass on the map and adjust the position of both, making sure that the compass needle still points to the top of the map and is parallel to the edge. By this method, the map is orientated in a north-south alignment. To find your position on the map, look out for prominent features and draw imaginary lines from them down on to the map. Your position is where these lines cross. This method of map reading takes a little practice before you can become proficient but it is worth the effort.

How to use this book

This book contains route maps and descriptions for 20 walks, with areas of interest indicated by symbols (see below). For each walk particular points of interest are denoted by a number both in the text and on the map (where the number appears in a circle). In the text the route instructions are prefixed by a capital letter. We recommend that you read the whole description, including the fact box at the start of each walk, before setting out.

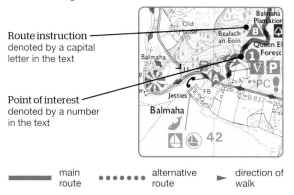

Route instruction denoted by a capital letter in the text

Point of interest denoted by a number in the text

▬▬▬ main route

•••••• alternative route

► direction of walk

Key to walk symbols

At the start of each walk there is a series of symbols that indicate particular areas of interest associated with the route.

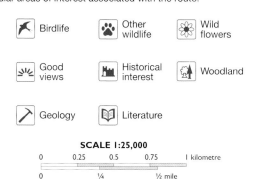

Birdlife

Other wildlife

Wild flowers

Good views

Historical interest

Woodland

Geology

Literature

SCALE 1:25,000

0   0.25   0.5   0.75   1 kilometre

0   ¼   ½ mile

Please note the scale for walk maps is 1:25,000 unless otherwise stated
North is always at the top of the page

> **A walk in the land of Rob Roy MacGregor, up Kirkton Glen and through plantations, before reaching stunning views from the open hillside pass**

Drivers on the main road between Strathyre and Lochearnhead often fail to notice peaceful Balquhidder Glen, let alone find Kirkton Glen, with its entrance hidden in dense plantations. Yet Kirkton Glen to Glen Dochart is an ancient through-route, well-known to the clansmen and tenant farmers of former days. The lower slopes of the glen are completely muffled by mature plantations. Nevertheless, give the forest just over an hour of your time in each direction for the rewards of the uplands beyond the conifer belt; this walk is only worth doing if you are prepared to go all the way, out of the forest and on to the upper valley. It offers varied birdlife, great views north and south, a cliff of some botanical interest, a transparent loch and superb rock scenery. The route starts from Balquhidder Church, where many visitors stop at the grave of Rob Roy MacGregor.

Rob Roy

Kirkton Glen

Loch Voil

Route instructions

A Park in Balquhidder. There are some spaces just below the churchyard, signed to Rob Roy's grave. Walk through the churchyard, pausing to read a little of its history in the church porch, then turn right, round the side of the church.

B From the church car park turn left, up a track, there is an information board by the car park. Turn right by the Forestry Commission Kirkton Glen sign.

C After about ten minutes walking, make sure you continue uphill, bearing slightly left on the main track. You will pass by the turning on the right for Craig an Tuirc, the viewpoint rock that overlooks the village.

1 Tiny goldcrests give the thinnest of squeakings from the tops of the Scots pine and larch. Look out for the larger (sparrow-sized) siskins, very handsome in green, black and yellow, which are common along this section.

D At the crossroads with the bridge on your left, go straight across, keeping the main stream to your left.

E All along this section, simply keep to the main track.

2 The first hint of a view, part of Meall an Fhiodhain, which you will ultimately stand under.

3 The view begins to open out into an amphitheatre

Crianlarich
Lochearnhead
Callander
Aberfoyle
Stirling
Helensburgh
Greenock
Cumbernauld
Kirkintilloch
Paisley
Glasgow
Motherwell

DISTANCE: 5 miles (8km), 1540ft (470m)

TIME: 2½ hours

START/END: NN535208 Balquhidder

TERRAIN: Moderate

MAPS:
OS Explorer 365;
OS Landranger 51 & 57

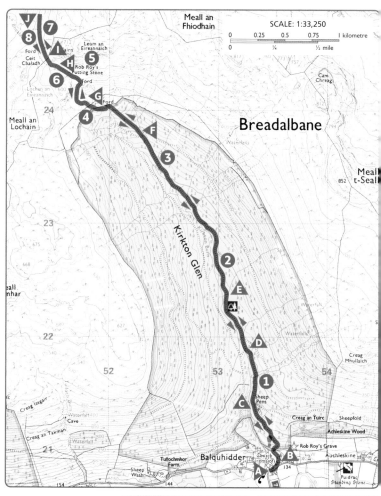

SCALE: 1:33,250

| 0 | 0.25 | 0.5 | 0.75 | 1 kilometre |

| 0 | ¼ | ½ mile |

Meall an Fhiodhain

Breadalbane

Kirkton Glen

Meall an Lochain

Meall t-Seal

of uplands. Leave the primroses alone!

F The track forks, take the right fork, then after a short time turn left leaving the forest road. This is clearly signed to Glen Dochart. You will have walked for at least an hour, unless very fit.

4 The relief at your escape from the plantation, plus the short, sharp slope, will mean you will pause to look down the glen at this point. Note Stuc a' Chroin to the left of Ben Ledi, the two most prominent peaks.

G At last you leave the forest and look out on to

Kirkton Glen

open uplands. Climb over the stile and follow the main path winding it's way up the hill to Rob Roy's Putting Stone.

5 In this lonely spot, huge blocks have fallen from the hollowed-out face above. This area is popular with rock climbers, but our route leads safely round the base. The huge rock at the base of Creag an Eireannaich, is known as 'Rob Roy's Putting Stone.' Legend has it that MacGregor and his men hid from their enemies here. Walkers can end their hike here (**H**) or continue onto the pass to enjoy views to the north.

H In order to gain a close view of the magnificent rocks of Meall an Fhiodhain, the most spectacular crag on the right, leave the path and cut right when below the middle craggy face to reach the base of the jumble of huge rocks. Walk on round the base of the rocks, north-westwards, until you rejoin the main path beyond the lochan.

6 On the left is the crystal-clear Lochan an Eireannaich – the little loch of the Irishman.

I On the main path, go through a gap in the broken fence but do not lose height as the view opens out northwards. Skirt a little way round the slope on your right for your final viewpoint. Expect to take at least one and a half hours to reach this, your furthest point.

7 Ben More is conspicuous westwards, sweeping up in a continuous rise from the main road running through Glen Dochart towards Crianlarich and the far west. There is a wide choice of 'Munros' – Ben Challum behind Crianlarich to the north-west, then, moving eastwards, Meall Glas and Sgiath Chuil are among the most identifiable of a complicated grouping of high hills, which are often known as the Mamlorn. From this point, Meall nan Tarmachan and Ben Lawers are obscured by the shoulder of Meall an Fhiodhain.

J Retrace your steps past the putting stone and to the main path back to the forest (**G**) and onto Balquhidder.

8 Observant walkers in April might note the low-growing cushions of purple saxifrage among the curiously eroded rocky hummocks. Many of Scotland's mountains are built of hard, acid rocks, such as quartzite or granite, with heather or crowberry dominant. But the widest variety of mountain plants prefer a basic rock like limestone or mica-schist.

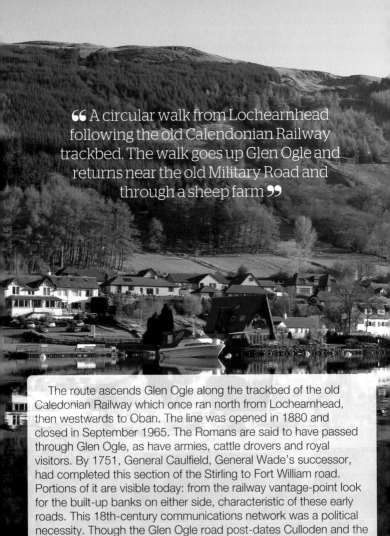

❝ A circular walk from Lochearnhead following the old Calendonian Railway trackbed. The walk goes up Glen Ogle and returns near the old Military Road and through a sheep farm **❞**

The route ascends Glen Ogle along the trackbed of the old Caledonian Railway which once ran north from Lochearnhead, then westwards to Oban. The line was opened in 1880 and closed in September 1965. The Romans are said to have passed through Glen Ogle, as have armies, cattle drovers and royal visitors. By 1751, General Caulfield, General Wade's successor, had completed this section of the Stirling to Fort William road. Portions of it are visible today: from the railway vantage-point look for the built-up banks on either side, characteristic of these early roads. This 18th-century communications network was a political necessity. Though the Glen Ogle road post-dates Culloden and the extinction of the Jacobite cause, a nervous government in London still found it wise to garrison the Highlands, moving troops by specially-built roads.

Queen Victoria, viewing the scene from her horse-drawn carriage in September 1842, remarked in her diary that the wildness reminded her of 'prints of the Kyber Pass'.

The Glen Ogle Railway Walk

Glen Ogle viaduct

Route instructions

A Park at the main Lochearnhead car-park on the A85, by the lochside, opposite the water sports centre.

B Walk back to the junction, then right towards the dismantled rail bridge beside the viaduct. This is not the railway you will walk. Cross the main road and look for a sign 'Lochearnhead Scout Station'.

C Turn left into the Scout Station then almost immediately turn right, indicated by the Glen Ogle Trail marker, climbing the bank above the entrance road. Go through the kissing gate then across the field on a clear path.

1 Half-way up the field, while pausing for breath you will notice the old Lochearnhead Station, now converted to a Scout Centre. This lay on the old Crieff-Lochearnhead line, closed in 1951. The disparity in height between the two lines meant their junction was two miles further south at Balquhidder.

D Turn right on trackbed.

2 At the trackbed, the view down Loch Earn stretches eastwards. This was considered, in its day, the finest view from a train anywhere in Britain, nearly 800ft (244m) up on the hillside. The bulk of Ben Our obscures parts of Ben Vorlich, but its neighbour

Plan your walk

DISTANCE: 6¼ miles (10km)

TIME: 3¼ hours

START/END: NN592237

TERRAIN: Moderate

MAPS:
OS Explorer 365;
OS Landranger 51 & 57

NOTE: As this walk goes through a sheep farm, dogs should not be taken.

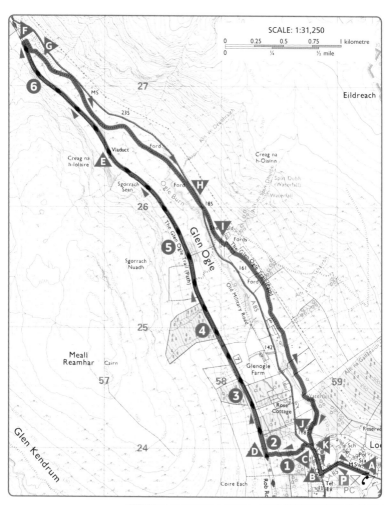

Stuc a' Chroin looks imposing.

3 Note the Scots pine – which have seen the railway come and go. Also obvious are the scrubby birches meeting overhead. These young trees have grown up since the railway disappeared. With the lineside fences originally in good order, sheep were excluded. The birches are a clear indication of the kind of tree regeneration which takes place when sheep are not present.

4 At bridge 104, note the scar of a new access road on the hillside opposite. The

The Glen Ogle Railway Walk

railway would have been equally conspicuous when it was first pushed through. Between this bridge and the next, look for signs of the old military road, now a green track running near the burn.

5 Between bridges 107 and 108, you will see evidence of the engineering problems: a rugged boulder-field above and left, that must have caused headaches for many a railway lengthman. A few scattered boulders on the trackbed in at least three places are slightly unsettling evidence of falls since the railway closed. Just below the viaduct can be seen different generations of engineers' efforts to stabilise the rockwalls, originally with stone, later with brick (note the cement dated 1946!).

E Take care on the viaduct.

6 Before finally leaving the railway, note, beyond the cutting, the military road below again, though there is a confusing section of old main road above it. Caulfield's work is nearest the stream. Compare the old hump-backed bridge with the later old road bridge above it, nearer the main road, and think of the manpower that brought these communications through, when the main tools were gunpowder, picks and shovels.

F Just beyond a footbridge, turn right over a stile following the clearly signposted Old Military Road to Lochearnhead. You are on your return journey.

G The top part of the path is faint but the general direction is clear, downhill between road and burn. You will eventually find a wide bit of old road, near the burn, probably a widened section of military road but now all grassed over.

H Note the alders growing in the stream bed. Cross a burn coming down from the left. The path then goes close to the road and crosses it beyond a gate. Watch for traffic.

I Your return is by following the postmarkers through fields and climbing a succession of stiles, staying parallel with the road. You bypass some outbuildings on their upper side before eventually dropping to the tree-lined stream bank.

J The Crieff-Lochearnhead railway viaduct is visible as you approach the stream crossing. Cross the footbridge and go through a gate near the electricity sub-station.

K Go through the kissing gate to main road and walk left, back into Lochearnhead.

66 A hard climb through mixed woodland to the Jubilee Cairn where rewarding views across Callander and the surrounding area await. A diversion on the return takes you to Bracklinn Falls 99

Callander Crags rise above Callander, looking almost inaccessible. Yet there are reasonable paths and rewarding views, far above the town. This walk also offers a diversion to the Bracklinn Falls, where Sir Walter Scott once rode his pony for a bet over the rickety bridge (now replaced! – a new bridge was opened in November 2010) that spans the Falls. Take care with children on the higher sections and at the Falls. The Queen Victoria Jubilee Cairn at the top of the Crags can also be reached by following the red waymarked route from the Forestry Commission car park.

The new footbridge over Bracklinn Falls

Callander Crags

River Teith with Callander Crags on the right

Route instructions

A Park in the Forestry Commission Callander Crags car park, from the A84 follow sign to Bracklinn Glen, car park on the left. From information board take level track straight ahead.

B Cross wooden footbridge, path splits, take left fork, going down the hill on slippery railway sleeper steps.

C Pass the Forestry Commission Crags sign, path goes right and starts to climb. Follow path upwards. Path becomes steep and can be slippery. Keep conifers on right and beech trees on left. Follow a ruined wall upwards, also on left. Turning left at Forestry Commission sign, takes you to Tulipan Crescent, the alternative parking place.

D Continue upwards with deer-proof fence on left.

E Cross small (and intermittent) stream and continue on.

1 First views of Ben Ledi, 2882ft (879m), north-westwards, and, to the south-east, Loch Venachar and the Menteith Hills.

F Continue along levelling path, noting steep path joining from right. Scramble across junction and follow fence on left to summit.

2 Good views over town from rocky ledge. Note St

Plan your walk

DISTANCE: 4 miles (6.5km), 890ft (273m)

TIME: 2 hours

START/END: NN633081

TERRAIN: Moderate

MAPS:
OS Explorer 365;
OS Landranger 57

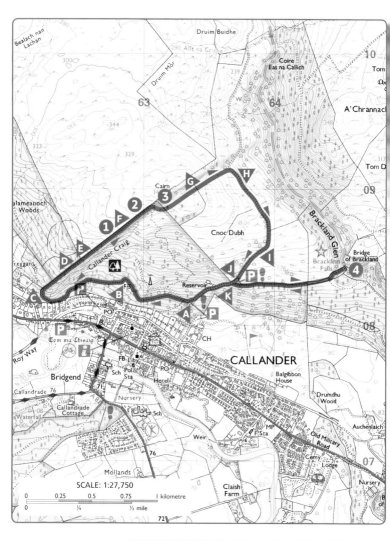

Kessog's Church, below, and the River Teith.

3 From the Queen Victoria Jubilee Cairn, erected in 1897 to celebrate Queen Victoria's Diamond Jubilee, there is a complete panorama: Ben Vorlich and Stuc a' Chroin northwards and (clockwise) Dumyat in the Ochils, the Wallace Monument and Stirling Castle, the Forth valley as far as the Pentlands, the Fintry Hills, the Menteith Hills, Ben Venue, Ben Ledi.

Callander Crags

G Continue eastwards keeping fence on left, losing height, the path is rough, rocky and muddy in places. Take care.

H With public road clearly in sight, go right, choosing path carefully over wet ground. Join road and turn right.

I Fifteen minutes later, there is a sign to the Red Well, a chalybeate (iron-rich) spring only moments from the road.

J At the Bracklinn Falls car park, turn left along clear path. Follow path to view Falls. Return to car park.

4 View from the bridge of spectacular Falls and mature mixed woodland of oak, ash and alder.

K Go left down the road and the starting point will eventually be reached.

Bracklinn Falls

66 An easy walk through oak woodland to the banks of the Garbh Uisge and the Falls of Leny *99*

The Falls of Leny are often visited from the north (or main A84 side) from a nearby car park on the A84. However, this delightful stroll visits them courtesy of the Callander-Oban Railway, the closure of which is much lamented. There are oak woods and wild water, birds and flowers to see in this short expedition. Take care with children, should you divert to the edge of the Falls. The extension suggested is a there-and-back-again walk eastwards towards Callander, and will interest birdwatchers in particular.

The track bed of the former railway is now an improved cycleway, part of a route from Glasgow via the Trossachs to Inverness. The walking is easy underfoot, with bridges and ramps making the Bridgend Cottage to Ben Ledi car park section suitable for pushchairs/wheelchairs.

Highland Cow at Kilmahog

Falls of Leny

Falls of Leny

Crianlarich   Lochearnhead

Callander

Aberfoyle

Stirling

Helensburgh   Cumbernauld
Greenock   Kirkintilloch

Paisley   Glasgow

Motherwell

DISTANCE: 2 miles (3.5km) with optional 3 mile (5km) extension

TIME: 1–2½ hours

START/END: NN586091

TERRAIN: Easy

MAPS:
OS Explorer OL 365;
OS Landranger 57

Route instructions

A Driving north from Callander on the A84, turn left at signpost for Strathyre Forest Cabins. Cross the bridge turn left onto the old track bed and park at the far end, near the parapet of the dismantled bridge.

B Leave the car park on the ramp at the parapet of the dismantled bridge, through the gate following route 7 cycle track signage. There is a path here, which is very well maintained and easy to follow. Follow this downstream.

1 Over the parapet of the dismantled bridge, look for grey wagtails, dippers and kingfishers.

C Make the most of this delightful level path and enjoy the bird-song in season and the cow-wheat, creeping jenny, violets and many other plants. The river at this point is called the Garbh Uisge, the 'rough water'. The path runs through attractive oak woodland

2 Corriechrombie, the 'bent birch corrie' is an old settlement upstream. Now upgraded to form a cycle and walking route, the path closely follows the old track which linked it with Callander and which pre-dates the military road and the railway.

D Rejoin the railway embankment near a second dismantled bridge. The falls are a little way downstream.

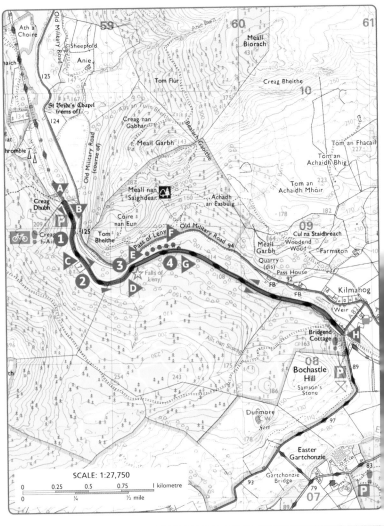

3 From the old parapet, looking north, note how the railway builders were forced to construct two bridges close together because of the difficult terrain, which has also squeezed the road and river together. Ben Ledi is ahead and the old charcoal burners' path is in the trees opposite and right.

E About 100yds (91m) after the bridges mentioned at **3**, near a stone seat like structure, take the path on

Falls of Leny

the left through the broken fence.

F Follow the path to the bank, then downstream. To view the Falls follow a faint path to the left, which ends above the Falls. The main path is faint in places, but continue parallel to the water's edge.

4 Note from the Falls the conspicuous and made-up path used by the less adventurous visitors on the far bank. Take care with small children; the bank here is steep.

G Follow a faint path to the right where you will rejoin the railway at a small bridge. Decide if you wish to retrace your steps or continue towards Kilmahog. It is about half an hour back to the car park from this point, if you turn right, back along the track bed to the parapet (**3**), then go left and retrace your steps. If you wish to lengthen the walk, go left. The path eventually meets the A821 (after about 30 minutes' walk) and this road makes a convenient turning point.

H Retrace your steps along the trackbed, going straight ahead at the small bridge mentioned in **G** and following outward path (left) at bridge parapet.

Garbh Uisge river

> **An easy walk into the Menteith Hills along the shore of Loch Venachar before climbing through conifers to reach an open moorland bowl**

The Highland Boundary Fault not only cuts across Loch Lomond, it also runs through Loch Venachar. Thus walkers on this path up the south side of Venachar are really in the beginnings of the lowlands, looking northwards into splendid Highland scenery. The path goes through conifer plantings then out into a moorland bowl, hemmed in by mini-crags to the north. Try it for an evening's ramble, to watch the sunset, giving the walk a couple of hours at least. Even walking boots are not essential, though (as ever) preferable. The path along Allt a' Chip Dhuibh can be very boggy in wet conditions.

Some walkers may wish to continue the walk to Aberfoyle. To return to Callander, check online for Demand Responsive Transport. This is a service provided by Stirling Council.

Loch Achray with

The Menteith Hills

Loch Venachar

Plan your walk

DISTANCE: 6 miles
(9.4km)

TIME: 3 hours

START/END: NN592056

TERRAIN: Easy

MAPS:
OS Explorer 365;
OS Landranger 57

Route instructions

A The path starts from the road to Invertrossachs House (private), reached by a turning off the A892. Park in the Invertrossachs estate car park after the first lodge, the road beyond is private. Return to the private lochside road and turn left heading along the shore of Loch Venachar.

B Go left and uphill where you see a sign 'Aberfoyle via Menteith Hills 5 miles'. The path goes momentarily left, then heads straight up through the birches (with the silver trunks) which grow in the firebreak.

1 Callander is seen eastwards on the right. Loch Venachar lies below and here is an end-on view of

Ben Ledi. Further west, Ben A'An (Walk 10) looms over the Trossachs gateway. Ben Venue is already beginning to disappear behind a nearby shoulder.

C The path rises gently, with an old wall below right.

D Path crosses a stream, then ascends a little ridge through dense forest, leaving the wall, before joining a forestry access road.

E Go right on forestry road. After a short distance turn left (at a passing place) and the path drops to the bank of the lochan.

2 Note the sheep pens below, disappearing in the

walk 5 The Menteith Hills 33

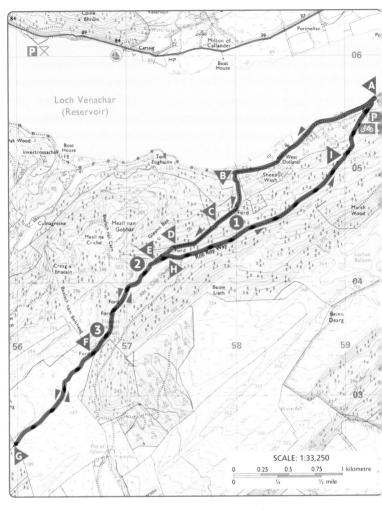

young trees. There is a lochan here, too, presumably formed by the damming of a marshy area by the forestry road.

3 A viewpoint southwards, Dumgoyne is the conspicuous hump on the edge of the Campsies.

F Go over ladder stile, over wall, opening into a moorland bowl.

G At second ladder-stile, note how the area beyond has been taken over for forestry, with some deciduous shelter planting around the right of way.

The Menteith Hills

This is a suggested turning point, though the path goes on, down into coniferous woodlands and on to Aberfoyle. Retrace your steps to .

Continue on forest road, ignoring footpath you came up. Keep left at the end of the dam.

Turn left and follow the forest road down to the car park.

Loch Venachar with Ben Ledi in the distance

Gaining its name, some authorities say, from the fortress of the Maeatae (Dun Maeatae), an ancient Pictish tribe, this hill may be lower than some of its more easterly neighbours in the Ochils, but its distinct dome makes it a landmark overlooking the Forth Valley. It is a popular walk for its extensive views. A public road enables the car-borne visitor to gain height easily, before reaching the car park. The temptation to come off the hill in a north-westerly direction and head towards a road and reservoir for a roundabout return should be resisted as this is not on any right of way (N.B. The name is pronounced 'Dim-aye-at' with the emphasis on the middle syllable.)

Dumyat has two summits principal summits, Dumyat to the east and Castle Law to the west, home of the remains of an ancient hill fort occupied by the Maeatae. Very few walkers visit Castle Law and this walk takes you to the main Dumyat summit.

66 A short walk up the most easterly peak in the Ochil Hills, affording spectacular views of the Forth Valley to the south and The Trossachs to the north 99

Dumyat

Plan your walk

View over the Forth Valley

Crianlarich · Lochearnhead
Callander
Aberfoyle
Stirling
Helensburgh · Cumbernauld
Greenock · Kirkintilloch
Paisley · Glasgow
Motherwell

Route instructions

A From the Stirling to Bridge of Allan road, the A9 (T), follow signs to Sheriffmuir, on the Bridge of Allan side of Stirling University campus. The road twists uphill until open moorland is reached. There is a car park on the right, near a pylon. At time of writing, a gate directs you onto the hillside.

B The path splits almost immediately. Continue on the level, taking the right fork.

1 Below and southwards are Stirling Castle and the Wallace Monument – already the views are extensive.

2 Note the two summits ahead. Left is Dumyat, right is Castle Law, the actual site of the fort.

C Another path wanders off to the right, towards the trees. Ignore it.

D Near signs of an old sheepfold (on the right) the path goes left and upwards, then gives a choice of up or round a heathery knoll.

E After the first boggy stream, keep steeply rising ground on left. Path points straight to the summit.

3 A momentary digression left will give a view of the ancient remains of the Castle Law fort. Two ruined walls are conspicuous (but flattened). The inner

DISTANCE: 3 miles (5km), 700ft (218m)

TIME: 1½ hours

START/END: NS813980

TERRAIN: Moderate

MAPS:
OS Explorer 366;
OS Landranger 57

NOTE: Keep your dog under strict control and on a lead – this is sheep country.

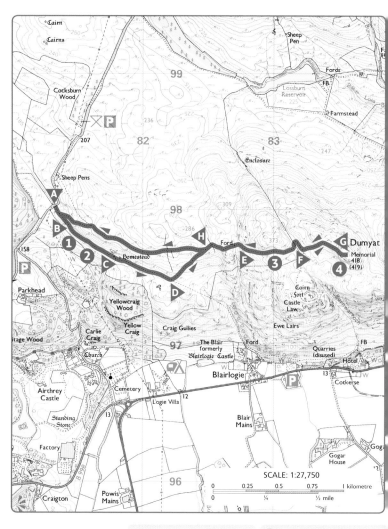

enclosure is thought to be later than these outer walls.

F Cross fence, or take left fork to stile to avoid boggy ground. The path is momentarily steep and rocky on its short pull to the top.

4 The Cleish Hills are far off to the east, the Pentlands are beyond the Forth Valley, but the views to the Trossachs hills are the most spectacular, with Ben Ledi, Ben Venue, Ben Vorlich, Stuc a' Chroin and Ben Lomond prominent.

Dumyat

G Retrace your steps to the back of the knoll mentioned at **D**.

H At its right-hand or western side, look for a path running off right which keeps to higher ground than the ascent path. Follow it until it rejoins the outward route at **B**, with the car park only a few yards further on.

Dumyat

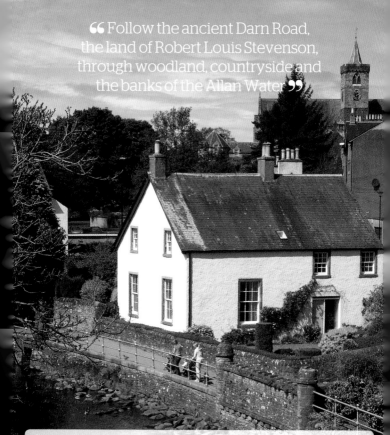

> **"** Follow the ancient Darn Road, the land of Robert Louis Stevenson, through woodland, countryside and the banks of the Allan Water **"**

This ancient way could have been the main road northwards in the early Christian era – armed Roman legions perhaps passed along it. Linking Dunblane and Bridge of Allan, it leads the visitor away from the hubbub of the A9 and through pleasantly wooded parkland, to a pretty riverside walk. As a child Robert Louis Stevenson spent time in Bridge of Allan when it was a spa town. The cave on the banks of the Allan Water is claimed to have given Stevenson inspiration for Ben Gunn's cave in *Treasure Island*. Small children should be watched on the banks of the Allan Water, and the Cock's Burn's gully needs a little respect.

This walk can be made into an A to B route, by continuing on the path after the old weir (▶) and then following the road down to Bridge of Allan, where a train can be caught back to Dunblane.

Allan Water in

The Darn Road

Route instructions

A Take the B8033 into Dunblane, cross the mini roundabout and go through the first set of lights and park in the parking places along this section of dual carriageway, near the police station.

B Cross the dual carriageway and look for signpost 'Footpath to Bridge of Allan 2½ Miles', near the bus stop.

Go up the slope and walk straight on along the edge of the golf course.

1 Viewpoint: glimpses of the Trossach hills on right and Gargunnock hills southwards across the parkland of Kippenross House.

C Path leaves edge of golf course with estate boundary wall on right and fence on left. Kippenross House is ahead, beyond the wall.

D Path continues in sheltered dip with walls on each side.

2 Look out for houses of Bridge of Allan and Stirling Castle appearing beyond the trees ahead.

3 Note giant redwood tree in plantation on left.

E Woodland on either side. The path runs under yews and drops to the Wharry Burn.

F Go over footbridge and

Plan your walk

DISTANCE: 4 miles (6.5km)

TIME: 2 hours

START/END: NN781010

TERRAIN: Easy

MAPS:
OS Explorer 366;
OS Landranger 57

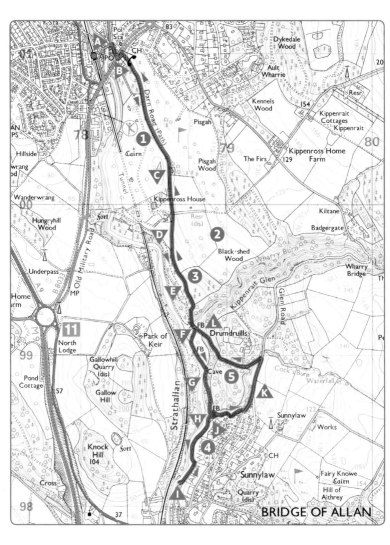

right to the banks of the Allan Water and walk downstream.

G Shortly after Allan Water footbridge (do not cross) Stevenson's Cave (associated with the author R.L. Stevenson), appears on left. Continue on the path which climbs the steepening bank.

H The gully of the Cock's Burn is crossed by a small footbridge. Take care here the path is narrow and

The Darn Road

slippery. Go up some steps then turn right to regain Darn Road for a 10 minute excursion downstream.

▶ Continue downstream to old weir and fish ladder. A small path goes through the trees to the old weir. Retrace your steps as far as the steps leading to Cock's Burn.

4 This viewpoint overlooks the Ladies' Pool, scene of a drowning accident in 1832. The Stirling Plain is southwards and the Victorian mansions of Bridge of Allan, built in its boom years as a spa, begin to appear to the south-east.

▶ Do not go down the steps to recross small footbridge. Go right and upstream to the public road.

▶ At road go left. Pass road merging from right, then shortly go left again, crossing the burn once again, following the signpost to the Darn Road. Go straight on at hilltop on to a track leading down to the left, NOT into private driveway to Drumdruills on right.

5 View southwards over woodland to the Stirling Plain.

▶ Return to Darn Road at Wharry Burn, an easy hour after you left it. Retrace your steps, over the footbridge, up and under the yews and on to Dunblane.

Robert Louis Stevenson's cave

> 66 A small mystical hill associated with Reverend Robert Kirk and home to the fairies 99

Doon Hill is associated with the 17th-century Gaelic scholar, the Reverend Robert Kirk, who investigated local fairy lore and published *The Secret Commonwealth* in 1691. As punishment for giving away the secrets of this Scottish supernatural world, he is said to have been spirited away to fairyland while walking on either this hill or Fairy Knowe nearby. The pine tree at the summit of this walk is said to contain the spirit of the minister. Evidence of 'the little folk' may be hard to find today, but evidence of the route is much simpler by following the way markers. Beautiful oaks, lots of bird song – an evening stroll in enchanted woodland, all within easy reach of Aberfoyle.

Around Doon Hill

Aberfoyle

Route instructions

A If driving west, immediately after the junction of the B829, to Stronachlachar, with the A821 (Duke's Pass) in Aberfoyle, turn left over a bridge and continue southwards over a second bridge and park where the road splits. Park on the left fork, near the sign for Doonhill Fairy Trail. Take the road straight ahead following the red way markers.

B Aberfoyle is on the left across the low river-meadows. Look for sign on right pointing to a smaller path left into wood. Take this clearly marked path, which goes uphill and right, eventually through short coniferous belt.

1 Note the bilberry and holly growing abundantly in the shelter of the oaks. If you are lucky you may see a red squirrel in the canopy.

C The summit views are restricted by the leafy canopy, but note the clouties hanging from branches and fairies left at the base of the trees. The route down heads off left (northwards) and is marked by red posts.

D At the bottom of the hill turn right onto a wider track that circles the base of the hill.

2 You have now left the waymarked route; to the left is birch with marshy meadows beyond while

Plan your walk

DISTANCE: 2 miles (3.5km)

TIME: 1 hour

START/END: NN518002

TERRAIN: Easy

MAPS:
OS Explorer 365;
OS Landranger 57

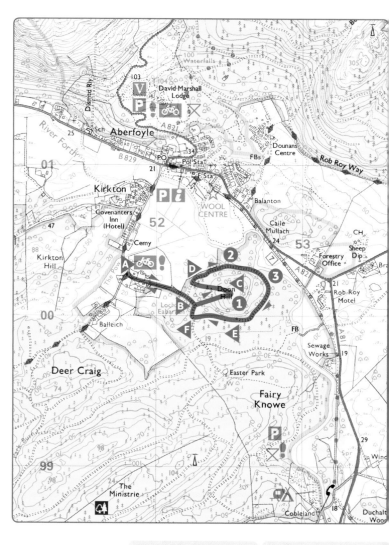

oaks cover the hill above and right. In spring listen hereabouts for snipe 'drumming' – making a strange resonant bleating sound with their specially-stiffened tail feathers held out against the air currents as they make their display flights. This difficult-to-locate noise carries a long way and is hard to relate to a highflying small bird. Listen for chiffchaffs repeating their own names in the oaks on the right.

Around Doon Hill

3 The river on the left is the Forth. Look out for grey wagtails, that is, any 'ordinary' or pied wagtail that shows creamy yellow below.

E The wide track fades away here, replaced by a vague footpath. If in doubt follow the base of the hill, now looking unexpectedly tall on the right.

F The path here is overgrown but heads straight through the broom to rejoin the forest road. Turn right and you will shortly join **B** to retrace your steps to the start.

Doon Hill circular path

> ❝ From the David Marshall Lodge to the
> Highland Boundary Fault, along forest
> roads and past pretty waterfalls ❞

Situated in the Queen Elizabeth Forest Park this walk starts from the David Marshall Lodge, a forestry visitor centre, gifted by the Carnegie Trust in 1960. There are a network of trails, information and a café available. *Go Ape* high wire forest adventure, is also located here. The Aberfoyle *Go Ape* boasts the longest zip wire in the UK. The walk follows forestry roads to Lime Craig where the route meets the Highland Boundary Fault, which was formed some 390 million years ago, this separates the boundary between the Scottish Highlands and Lowlands. The walk passes mostly through conifer plantations where red squirrels are found, and, in the autumn, numerous wild mushrooms.

Lochan Reoidhte offers an extension to the walk

Lime Craig & Highland Boundary Fault

David Marshall Lodge

Plan your walk

DISTANCE: 4 miles (6.5km), 1020ft (310m)

TIME: 2 hours

START/END: NN518014

TERRAIN: Moderate

MAPS:
OS Explorer 365;
OS Landranger 57

Route instructions

A Park in the Forestry Commission's car park at David Marshall Lodge, on the A821 north of Aberfoyle. The walk starts from the eastern corner of the Lochan and at the time of writing followed the blue waymarks for the majority of the route. Take the path opposite the information board, and continue straight on at the first junction.

B Take right path down to the river.

1 Note the sculptures camouflaged in the wood.

2 Leave the path briefly to admire the waterfall on your left.

C Cross river over bridge, turn left climbing forest road.

3 There is a squirrel hide hidden in the trees, if you are lucky you will see one of the many red squirrels in the area and some birdlife. To explore descend the wooden steps and follow the broadwalk to the hide.

D Keep left, climbing the forest road you will pass *Go Ape*, forest walkways high in the canopy, left.

4 On the left is a second waterfall and bench overlooking it.

E At crossroads take right junction.

5 On the right is a bench and viewpoint overlooking

walk 9 Lime Craig & Highland Boundary Fault   49

Aberfoyle and across to Doon Hill (Walk 8) and the hills to the south – Dumgoyne and the Campsies.

F End of the forest road, continue straight ahead, up the steep rough path, waymarked with a red sign and a Forestry Commission view point sign. If you do not wish to climb Lime Craig go to **I**.

G Follow path round to the right, then turn right on forestry road to the summit.

Lime Craig & Highland Boundary Fault

6 There are views in all directions, to the north Ben Ledi (then anti-clockwise), Ben Vane and Glen Finglas can be seen. The slopes of Ben A'an (Walk 10) can be seen but not the summit, Ben Venue further west, coming round to the local Craigmore above the David Marshall Lodge, where the walk started. Ben Lomond to the west, with the distinctive Dumgoyne to the south on the edge of the Campsies and Fintry Hills, Flanders Moss and the Carse of Stirling and the Gargunnock Hills, and finally to the east and above you the Menteith Hills.

Retrace your steps to **F**.

Take the path on the left, descending the hill. You rejoin the blue way marked route here.

At the bottom of the descent turn right on the forest road.

Left on a smaller path, signposted for David Marshall Lodge. Cross the river on the wooden bridge and turn right.

Left then almost immediately right, climbing the hill back to the David Marshall Lodge, which is worth a visit before returning to the car.

Bluebell woods

❝ A steep hard climb with rewarding views over Loch Katrine and to the east from the summit ❞

Ben A'an is, in mountain terms, not particularly high – a mere 1520ft (454m). But it fits into the general scheme of the Trossachs very well giving the impression of rugged, almost unapproachable, grandeur in spite of its small scale. It makes a pleasant afternoon's walk for the fit and well-shod, though the last section is steep. The route described here is of the there-and-back-again variety, but its view makes it amply rewarding. Over the last few years a path has become increasingly conspicuous leading off the summit crags north-west and turning down towards the shore of Loch Katrine; please disregard it, as Scottish Water prefers that you return the way you came up. Besides, the forbidden path is slippery, vague and blocked by fallen trees. Climb Ben A'an on a clear day and the panorama, except to the north, is stunning.

Ben A'an – A Trossachs View

Views from the summit of Ben A'an in winter

Route instructions

A The path starts opposite the car park a little west of the holiday property bond Tigh Mor Trossachs, near the west end of Loch Achray. It is rocky and climbs relentlessly, through larch plantations.

B Take the steepest route, straight ahead!

C Going up the rocky bank of the Allt Inneir burn (on your right) the path is rough, cross the stream via the wooden footbridge.

1 Just before you are hemmed in on both sides by the trees, look back over Loch Achray. You can see the Duke's Pass climbing the hill before heading onto the David Marshall Lodge and Aberfoyle.

D The stream is now in the trees and can be heard on your left. Shortly afterwards there is a clearing with splendid views down Loch Achray. The path continues at the far end of the clearing and shortly crosses the stream again.

E Out of the trees, a conspicuous knoll is seen on the left. Divert for a foretaste of the view further up, then rejoin the path. The path becomes steep and rocky from here on. N.B. if any members of the party are uneasy about the short, steep section seen ahead and to the right of Ben A'an's cone; then they could happily wait at this point for the party's return.

Plan your walk

DISTANCE: 2 miles (3.5km), 1200ft (360m)

TIME: 1 hour

START/END: NN509070

TERRAIN: Strenuous

MAPS:
OS Explorer 365;
OS Landranger 57

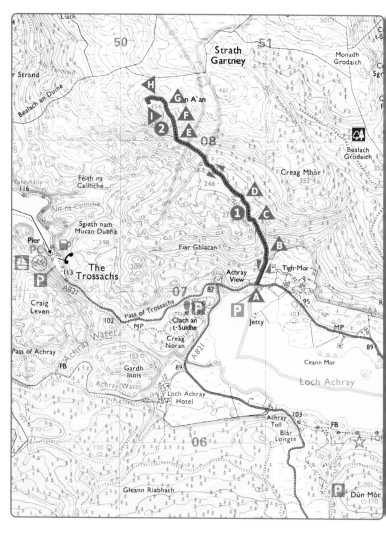

F▸ Take care as the path
reaches the base of the
cone, as it can be slippery.
Note the little path going
off left to the base of the
rocks, for the benefit of
rock climbers. Ignore it,
as you take the main right

fork and find yourself with
a stiff upward pull, on a
steep path which has
small steps in places.

G▸ You share your upward
route with a stream.

Ben A'an – A Trossachs View

H Do not be tempted by a seeming shortcut on the left through a cleft, as the path begins mercifully to flatten out. Continue round to the col behind the main peak, as this is a safer route.

▶ Retrace your steps, taking care on the steep descent.

2 After you wind round to the summit, take care on the steep southern face that suddenly appears at your feet. The full length of Loch Katrine spreads westwards. To the south, the lowland hills are conspicuous: Dumgoyne on the edge of the Campsies, then the Fintry and Gargunnock Hills. Beyond Loch Achray, below, and Loch Venachar, behind, Dumyat (Walk 6) in the Ochils is another conspicuous top in the east, with the Forth Valley misty in the far south-east. Ben Ledi, then, further west, Ben More, Stob Binnein and a range of Perthshire hills are conspicuous. In line with the northern shore of Katrine, but quite far to the north-west is the triangle of Ben Lui. To complete the view, more high peaks west of Loch Lomond can be seen, among them the distinctive craggy top of The Cobbler. Ben Lomond looms round the right edge of nearby Ben Venue.

Loch Katrine from the summit of Ben A'an

Most of today's visitors are decidedly unfamiliar with the literary output of Sir Walter Scott. Hence the landmarks of *The Lady of the Lake*, his long narrative poem, are much less studiously sought out than they once were. The 'wild and strange retreat' of Ellen Douglas, in the third canto, is set in Coire nan Uruisgean, which today's maps still faithfully mark as the Goblins' Cave. It is conspicuous from the Scottish Water road that runs along Loch Katrine's north bank, or from Ben A'an (Walk 10), and is a gash and a rockfall on the slopes of Ben Venue. It lies on the wildest part of Loch Katrine's shores, reached by the Bealach nam Bo – the pass of the cattle – a name with historical rather than literary overtones. The main drove road for cattle from the west lay along the south shore of Katrine. This short walk traverses part of it.

The Loch Katrine Dam

From the dam looking out towards Loch Katrine

Route instructions

A Park in the Forestry Commission Ben Venue car park opposite the shore of Loch Achray on A821. Turn right down the A821 for 440yds (400m).

B Turn right towards the Loch Achray Hotel, follow the road around the back of the hotel, cross the bridge and continue on the forest road climbing gently.

C Take right fork at wide forestry road junction.

D Continue straight on.

1 The Bealach nam Bo appears as a notch on the skyline ahead.

E Continue straight on.

F Go over a ladder-stile at a high fence. The path follows a fence on the right and is extremely boggy here in wet conditions; keep to the pass straight ahead.

G If short of time the second fence with its gap for a gate is your turning point. Continue from **K**.

H If continuing for a closer view of the bealach and Loch Katrine. Go through gap. The path now becomes rough and stoney and has a stream on the right, but shortly crosses it, continuing to keep to the lowest point in the temporarily narrowing valley.

I Divert right to knoll, a few yards away.

Plan your walk

DISTANCE: 3 miles (5km) with optional strenuous 1 mile (1.5km) extension

TIME: 1½-2 hours

START/END: NN506068

TERRAIN: Easy

MAPS:
OS Explorer 365;
OS Landranger 57

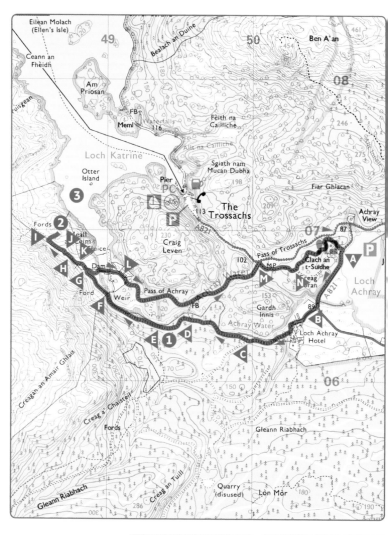

2 View of the amphitheatre that opens out ahead of you. Ahead looms the pass, with its dramatic rock fall and solitary tree against the skyline. Below right is Loch Katrine with the Scottish Water road snaking along the opposite shore. In the summer season the steamship *Sir Walter Scott* may float into view to make the perfect picture. Do not be tempted by the path ahead. It goes as far as a gate on the far side

The Loch Katrine Dam

of the enclosure, then the path deteriorates to make the pass no place for the leisurely walker.

3 Loch Katrine holds 14,212 million gallons of water, largely the result of the average annual rainfall of 84.4 inches (2150mm) on the loch itself. It supplies Glasgow's water.

J Return to the gap in the fence.

K As you go through the gap, you will see a stile, left. Go over stile and turn right, downwards, following path around the bottom of

a rocky outcrop to the dam. Take care if children are present. Cross the dam.

L Go right, past the dwelling house, on to the tarmac road. Keep to the road.

M Go through white gate and just before main road turn right and follow broadwalk over boggy ground.

N Turn left and the path will take you back to the car park. The right path also takes you back to the car park.

Achray Water

> **A walk along the south shore of Loch Ard, Ben Lomond can be seen in the distance before returning through forestry plantations**

This walk follows the south shore of Loch Ard, on a variety of forest roads and smaller paths. It then leaves the loch climbing up through plantations to a fine view of the loch before joining the Lochard cycle route to return to Milton via the pretty Lochan Ghleannain. A good walk for a windy day as the trees give shelter. The walk follows one of the many sculpture trails in the area, where there are sound posts featuring native wildlife sounds and a narrative recorded by the local primary school. There are various sculptures along the loch side and a collection of unusual seats and shelters which incorporate interactive activities. These all make for an enjoyable and educational walk for the family. At the time of writing, this walk was waymarked by red markers.

There are endless opportunities to extend this walk, one extension is possible by following the waymarked lowest track westward to Kinlochard, returning by a loop, but in places the views are severely curtailed and the way made monotonous by endless conifers.

A way marker on the path

Loch Ard Forest

Loch Ard

Route instructions

 On the B829 Aberfoyle-Stronachlachar road, turn left at Milton, at the clearly signposted Loch Ard Forest. Over the bridge then turn right and follow the signs to the Forestry Commission Milton car park. Leave the car park and turn right down the road you drove up.

 Turn left towards Loch Ard.

 Go through the gate and past the cottage called Lochend, to reach the narrows of Loch Ard on their way to becoming the River Forth, a surprisingly domestic scene with boathouses and swans.

D At the fork, keep to the lower track on the right,

waymarked at time of writing.

1 The first sculpture and Ben Lomond dominates the western horizon in this view of Little Loch Ard. Note also Helen's Rock, a face dropping steeply into the loch on the opposite bank. This is also known as Echo Rock because of the remarkable acoustic properties hereabouts.

E Leave the forest road, turn right on a smaller path which follows the shores of the Loch on a path with short steep climbs. Rob Roy's Cave is on the left but now hidden by trees.

2 Another peaceful spot by the water's edge, this

Plan your walk

DISTANCE: 3¾ miles (6km)

TIME: 2 hours

START/END: NN498011

TERRAIN: Easy

MAPS:
OS Explorer 365;
OS Landranger 57

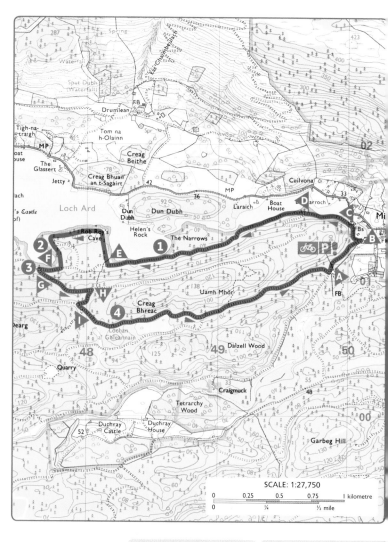

time giving a full-length view of the loch. (Approach quietly in spring to hear the frogs' croak!) Note Ledard Glen on the far shore. Listen for the cackle of jays, too, a species of patchy distribution in Scotland, though benefiting from the kind of intensive forestry in which you are now standing.

F Note the waterside viewpoint across the Loch. Turn right and rejoin the forest road.

Loch Ard Forest

3 Note the sculptured squirrels in the trees.

G Turn left, signposted Milton car park, gently climbing the hill. If continuing to Kinlochard carry straight on.

H Follow the track round to the right.

Turn left and climb gently up hill, follow this road back to Milton Car Park and the start.

4 Stop at the highpoint and appreciate the views ahead with the pretty Lochan Ghleannain below.

Loch Ard Forest

> 66 A walk along the shores of Loch Katrine, before climbing a rough hillside to follow the line of the aqueduct and finally descending to the picturesque Loch Arklet 99

This walk follows the line, above ground, of a tunnel bored through the ridge that separates Loch Katrine from Loch Chon. It carries Glasgow's water supply on the start of its 26 mile (42km) journey from Loch Katrine and was started in 1855. Royal Cottage, which the walk skirts, is the draw-off point and was so named from Queen Victoria's visit in 1859 to open the works officially. The first part is along a metalled road with delightful views. Once over the rough ground of the ridge, the return walk is by a recently built cycle track, with fine views of Loch Arklet. This is one of the most scenic routes to walk anywhere in the Trossachs. The solitude of the high ground is in contrast to the scene in the 1850s, when the area swarmed with gangs of navvies. Please note that the shafts mentioned along the length of tunnel are more strictly towers and it is quite impossible to see into them, let alone fall down them.

View north across
Loch Katrine

Loch Katrine & the start of the Aqueduct

Steamship *Sir Walter Scott* preparing to sail to Stronachlacher

Plan your walk

Crianlarich · Lochearnhead · Callander · Aberfoyle · Stirling · Helensburgh · Greenock · Cumbernauld · Kirkintilloch · Paisley · Glasgow · Motherwell

DISTANCE: 4½ miles (7.5km)

TIME: 2¼ hours

START/END: NN404102

TERRAIN: Moderate

MAPS:
OS Explorer 364;
OS Landranger 50 & 56

Route instructions

A If driving, go right at the western junction of the B829 and park at the Stronachlachar car park, where the steamer calls. Go back up the drive, turn left, then second left to gain the road that runs along the south bank of Loch Katrine. The sign says 'Private Road, No Unauthorised Vehicles'.

1 The supply from Loch Arklet over the hill, right, drops down to the main reservoir, via a series of quite impressive, though entirely artificial, cascades dating from 1895. Looking the other way, Factor's Island lies just off the Stronachlachar pier, while in the east Ben A'an's distinctive hump marks the heart of the Trossachs.

B Continue along this picturesque surfaced road. It carries only Scottish Water traffic and follows the old drove road down Glen Gyle (at the far west end of Katrine) and over the Bealach nam Bo. Note, left, the hill passes on the far shore which the Macgregors would have used to travel to upper Balquhidder.

2 An open, ever-changing view of hill and loch. Cameras at the ready.

3 Just before leaving the surfaced road, look back, west, across the loch where both Portnellan and Glengyle House can be seen. Each has associations with the Macgregors.

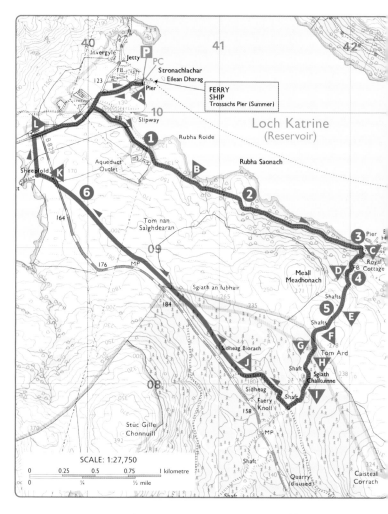

C Just before the green fence and wall, turn right and join a track that goes up and joins a stream on your left.

D Cross over stream.

4 As you cross, look for the conspicuous shaft of the outgoing aqueduct.

This looks like a circular, blank, stone-built tower. Beneath your feet are two tunnels, each of about 1½ miles (2.4km) length, taking water gently towards Frenich at the end of Loch Chon. Look up to the skyline, where a slightly surreal collection of other

Loch Katrine & the start of the Aqueduct

tower-like structures marks the course of this Victorian engineering feat.

5 To reach this optional viewpoint, leave the path momentarily at an inconspicuous fork. The main path skirts the topmost knoll to the right, but on top, near another obelisk, there is a fine view towards the Balquhidder peaks, northwards, and an unexpected view of Ben Lomond to the south. Loch Arklet lies to the west.

E After a short wettish section, go past a strange obelisk, devoid of any markings, presumably an aid to surveying the line of the tunnel. The path kinks uphill here.

F Follow the path round to the right or climb the knoll – the heathery descent is slippery and steep.

G Go through the kissing gate and into the coniferous plantation.

H At the first shaft in the forest, take care to follow the path going left and into the woodland. This avoids the slippery slope beyond the shaft.

I Follow the path back to the forest road, turn right.

J Turn right along the cycle track, about 110yds (100m) before the B829.

6 A splendid end-on view of Loch Arklet. This view must be one of the most constantly-changing in all the Highlands. Loch Lomond, lying out of sight beyond the end of Arklet, can often be in squalls, while the nearer loch is flooded with sunlight. Arklet itself was increased to three times its size in order to supplement supplies from Loch Katrine. While looking down this lonely glen, consider that in Rob Roy's day, there was a township of around twenty houses at Corriearklet, the settlement on the northern bank.

K Cross road and continue on the cycle track.

L Turn right, follow road to retrace steps to start.

View from Meall Meadhonach, the hill behind Royal Cottage

> 66 A walk through forest plantations to a ruined hamlet before heading home via the West Highland Way and native oaks 99

Sample the famous banks of Loch Lomond without committing too much energy and time to the excursion. First-time visitors along this section of the Balmaha-Rowardennan road will find the celebrated shoreline an interesting combination of private property and public recreation areas, which caused some headaches for the planners of the West Highland Way. This little walk takes advantage of part of a forestry trail, then joins the West Highland Way for the return. Take care, though, on slippery treeroots in the plantation and also near the viewpoint on the banks of Loch Lomond. Enjoy the birdsong of the oakwoods – from May onwards, dedicated birdwatchers will be sorting out the songs of wood warbler, garden warbler, redstart and tree-pipit, while the rest of the party will be enjoying the views across to Inchlonaig – the island of the yew trees, which were said to have been planted by Robert the Bruce to supply the Scottish bowmen.

Sallochy Wood & the banks of Loch Lomond

Wester Sallochy ruins

Route instructions

A On the continuation of the B837, 4 miles (6.4km) north of Balmaha, look for the road signs to the Sallochy Wood car park, your starting point. Park and follow the path away from the loch and across the road, noting the change of woodland into managed plantation. The route is waymarked with blue and red markers at the starting point.

B Bear right at the first path junction, away from the stream.

C Bear right on the main path at the top of the hill, ignore the track below the telegraph poles.

D You pass the ruined hamlet of Wester Sallochy,

swamped by gloomy conifers. Follow the path left, twisting past the old walls, then go right and up.

E You emerge on to a forestry road. If you turn left at the forest road, it takes you to higher viewpoints beyond an old quarry, seen on the left. Instead, go right on the forestry track.

1 Strathcashel Point is in view as you stroll gently down the track.

F Cross the main road and on the shore side, look for a faint track, almost opposite heading down to the water's edge.

G The path soon joins the West Highland Way. Go right.

DISTANCE: 2½ miles (4km)

TIME: 1¼ hours

START/END: NS380958

TERRAIN: Easy

MAPS:
OS Explorer 347 & 364;
OS Landranger 56

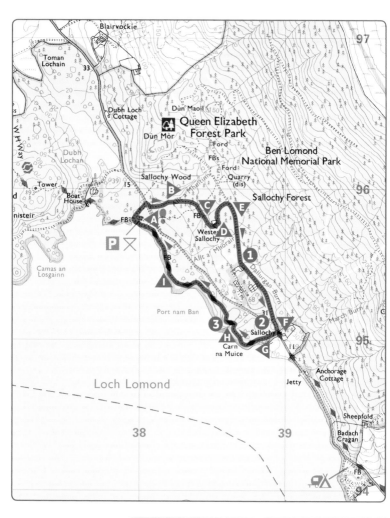

2 Very pleasing, open woodland with honeysuckle underfoot.

H To avoid a rocky outcrop, the path kinks right and up.

3 A splendid viewpoint south to Inchlonaig and the other islands beyond. Luss is the village on the far bank. In summer, note the dense oak canopy immediately below. On the shore, peeping sandpipers are common in spring before too many visitors arrive.

▶ Enjoy this well-maintained section back to the car park.

Sallochy Wood & the banks of Loch Lomond

West Highland Way

Conic Hill rises behind Balmaha on Loch Lomond. Though higher, it seems to match the shape of the islands that rise in a line from it out into the loch. Geologically, this is unsurprising as Conic Hill and the islands lie on the Highland Boundary Fault. Stand on its summit and you can truly look on two different landscapes and cultures. The conglomerate rock of which the hill is constructed is a great geological pudding-mix. A red sandstone matrix holds together stained and water-rounded pebbles of various sizes, commonly of quartz and associated with the fault line. It can be a little treacherous to walk over; take care while descending the slope on the last of the hill's convex humps. There are continuous views all the way from the top of the pass and the walk is naturally most rewarding in clear weather.

> 66 A lovely walk to the top of Conic Hill, where there are stunning views in all directions 99

Loch Lomond from the summit of Conic Hill

Conic Hill

Conic Hill

Route instructions

A There is a large car park in Balmaha, on the right going north. The walk starts from behind it, by the Forestry Commission sign. Go on to a forestry track and turn right.

1 Self-heal is the small purplish flower with a dense head. St John's Wort is taller, about 12 inches (30cm), with several yellow starry flowerheads. They grow along the track in high summer.

B Turn left, follow West Highland Way arrows.

2 Listen for the thin high mewing of buzzards calling! They are common on the moorland around the hill.

C Go through kissing gate, noting lambing notices.

3 The distinct texture of the conglomerate rock is already apparent on the hill shoulder ahead. Note Stockie Muir in the distance, right, with the rocky line of the approach to The Whangie (Walk 19). The nearer dome of Duncryne Hill (Walk 18) at the south end of Loch Lomond is conspicuous behind the marshes of the Endrick mouth.

D The path, which started level, bends upwards and left by way of some steps. Cross the stream at the top of the slope.

4 As the path flattens out, there are the first views

Plan your walk

Crianlarich
Lochearnhead
Callander
Aberfoyle
Stirling
Helensburgh
Greenock
Cumbernauld
Kirkintilloch
Paisley
Glasgow
Motherwell

DISTANCE: 3 miles (5km), 1130ft (345m)

TIME: 1½ hours

START/END: NS421909

TERRAIN: Strenuous

MAPS:
OS Explorer 347;
OS Landranger 56

NOTE: During the lambing season, from April to May, dogs are not allowed.

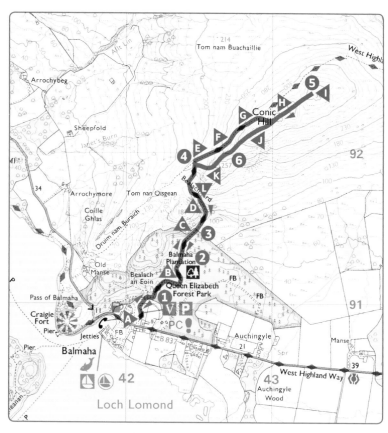

over long moorland slopes towards Ben Lomond, left, with the Arrochar Hills beyond, on the other side of the loch. Almost immediately, look for a short pathway joining from the heights above right. This is where you will rejoin later.

E Make your way round to the top of the 'bealach' or pass.

F Keep to the waymarked path while it continues to ascend gently, with the bulk of the hill blocking all views on the right.

G At the highest point of the West Highland Way proper leave it for a smaller path that goes up and right on to a little pass between two areas of higher ground. Go left aiming for the highest point.

H At the summit continue along the ridge on a faint and intermittent path, walking away from Loch Lomond. Climb two small

Conic Hill

hills. At the second, there is a small cairn. This is the most easterly high top of Conic Hill.

5 From this top there are two tops visible looking back south-west, as well as a wide prospect of Loch Lomond itself. Look beyond the islands in line; in clear conditions the hills of Arran are visible beyond the Clyde, a distance of more than 40 miles (65km). In the opposite direction, try to pick out the Wallace Monument, on its crag beside Stirling. Southwards, the towerblocks of Glasgow can also be seen, between the Kilpatricks and the Campsies. There are Highlands to the right and lowlands to the left – a very obvious contrast in landscapes.

▶ Retrace your steps along the ridge westwards along the line of the tops. (They can be a little confusing – there usually seems to be one more than you expect!) Note as you set off that the next top but one seems about the same height as your departure point. There are, however, four of roughly the same height.

▶ Take great care on this lower top, where the path is lost among the knobbly rock. You will see the West Highland Way just below you.

6 A last view of the islands without tops intruding. Inchcailloch is nearest, with Clairinsh just to the left, then, going out, Torrinch, Creinch and Inchmurrin. Notice how Ben Bowie on the far bank also lines up, marking the fault line. But it was the much more recent Ice Age, only ending 10,000 years ago, that carved out the loch in front of you, scouring a deep (600ft; 183m) trench in the schists to the north, then broadening out where it met the lowland sandstones to form a shallower lowland loch of only around 75ft (23m) depth. The dumped material from the glacier has kept the sea out, but Loch Lomond is only 27ft (8m) above sea level. Just as the Inveruglas Water (Loch Sloy) once drained eastwards, so the rivers in Glen Douglas and Glen Luss (up the loch on the far bank) once drained eastwards into the valley now occupied by the Endrick, until the Loch Lomond glacier cut through their courses. Now the Endrick flows west.

▶ Join the main path by going off right, at the top of the bealach.

▶ Retrace your steps to the car park.

This walk is a little different from the others: it is on an island. You can walk round the island in just over an hour (it is bigger than it first appears) but it is suggested you spend, at the very least, two hours, to soak up the atmosphere, enjoy the superb summit views, picnic, take pictures etc. There are two walking routes on the island – the Low Path and the Summit Path. This walk takes the latter route and there are a series of posts along the route which relate to the trail guide – *A Walking Guide to Inchcailloch*.

Inchcailloch is managed by Loch Lomond and the Trossachs National Park and the greatest respect must be paid to its woodlands: keep to the paths, keep your dog under the strictest control, and read the notice on landing.

Inchcailloch, Loch Lomond National Nature Reserve

View from Inchcailloch looking north

Plan your walk

DISTANCE: 2½ miles (4km)

TIME: 1¼ hours

START/END: NS421909

TERRAIN: Moderate

MAPS:
OS Explorer 347;
OS Landranger 56

NOTE: Camping is possible at Port Bawn. Seek permission from the National Park Centre in Balloch (01389 722600).

Route instructions

A Park in the main Balmaha car park, on the right going north. Go back and cross the main road. Opposite is a road down to the loch. Go down the road, turning right for the pier and the departure point.

Inchcailloch can be reached by using the services of *MacFarlane and Son*, The Boatyard, Balmaha, Loch Lomond, G63 0JG, Tel: (01360) 870214 or visit www.balmahaboatyard. co.uk. They run an on-demand ferry service to Inchcailloch, in addition to cruises on the loch, which also call at Inchcailloch by arrangement. Phone them with the numbers in your party and arrange a suitable time. The island

can also be reached from the west shore of the loch with *Cruise Loch Lomond*. They operate a daily scheduled service from Luss on their 'Wee Gem' cruise. This runs from April to 2nd October departing from Luss Pier, visit www. cruiselochlomond.co.uk.

B Disembark at North Bay and follow the path straight up from the jetty.

C Turn left and cross a stream by a footbridge.

D The oaks are replaced by alder trees where it is wet. Note how these alders have several trunks, suggesting they have been coppiced some time ago. Keep on the main path.

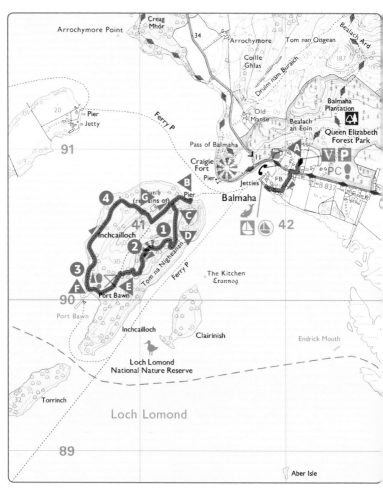

1 On your way to this viewpoint, there is a face of the lumpy conglomerate sandstone (familiar if you have already walked on Conic Hill). Higher up you look south to the island of Clairinsh (with its 'crannog', a 2000-year-old, manmade island at its left-most tip) and beyond to the Endrick marshes. Behind these are the Fintry Hills then (right), the Campsies and the Kilpatricks.

2 But an even better view is to follow, looking north to the Highlands from the 250ft (75m) high summit: a huge panorama of island and mountain.

Inchcailloch, Loch Lomond National Nature Reserve

The path leads down to a junction. (There is the remains of a corn-drying kiln on the right of the path just before the junction, at the foot of the slope; it looks like an old drain.) Go left to the slightly unexpected camp-site at Port Bawn then back along the shore.

Take a left turn if you wish to visit Port Bawn. There are composting toilets here.

3 Like Conic Hill, Inchcailloch has a band of serpentine running parallel to and north of the fault line. This metamorphic rock, seen in an outcrop just left of the path, looks dingy and is smoother than the conglomerate.

4 The site of Inchcailloch Farm. Although the entire island, thickly wooded, looks natural, the oaks are mature trees that have grown up from the managed woodland which was a source of oak bark, used in the tanning industry. This stage in the history of Inchcailloch was from about 1770 till the end of the 19th century. Before that, the island was farmed; the Nature Conservancy Council's nature trail booklet gives further information.

Veer right and uphill to the 13th-century church,

evidence of the vanished community. From here it is only a few minutes walk down left, then left again, back to the shore and the landing stage on the right.

Inchcailloch

One of the easiest walks in this book, Gartocharn, bypassed by most of the tourist hurly burly, sits contentedly in a patchwork of little fields. An important feature of the walk is its little foray into Shore Wood, part of the Loch Lomond National Nature Reserve. The reserve consists of five islands – Creinch, Torrinch, Clairinsh, Aber Isle and Inchcailloch, all clearly seen from the shore – and a substantial part of the marshes around the mouth of the Endrick Water. Please note, only a part of Shore Wood is open without permission and it is important to keep strictly to the shore path.

66 A pleasant walk across farmland and along country lanes before reaching the shores of Loch Lomond National Nature Reserve 99

Gartocharn & the banks of Loch Lomond

Gartocharn with Ben Lomond behind

Plan your walk

DISTANCE: 3½ miles (5.5km)

TIME: 1¾ hours

START/END: NS428863

TERRAIN: Easy

MAPS:
OS Explorer 347;
OS Landranger 56

Route instructions

A Gartocharn is on the A811 south of Loch Lomond. Park sensibly in the village; there is some parking near the church, reached by turning left (if coming from Balloch) opposite the House of Darrach and following the road round to the right past the Police Station. The community centre is beyond the church to the east. Park, then go past the community centre and turn immediately left down the track beside the centre. Go through a gate.

1 Immediately a view of Loch Lomond opens up. Note the craft moored at Balmaha on the right-hand side of the loch and Ben Lomond dominating beyond.

B Follow a faint track down through the field, keeping the boundary hedge on your right.

C Go through the gate and follow the path through the enclosure. A stream appears on the left.

D Go through the gate and follow field boundary on your left until you reach a gate and a bridge on your left.

E The path goes down a short track, over a second little bridge and through a gate on to a surfaced road. Turn right, then left at end of road.

F Look for a small postbox only about 100yds (91m) further on. Turn right

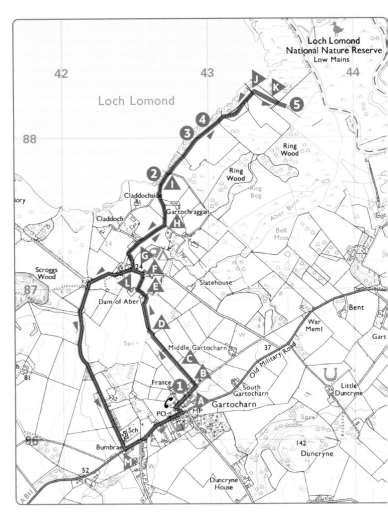

down track signed as Loch Lomond National Nature Reserve.

G At first junction, go straight on.

H At next junction take left fork and follow the track down to the bank of the loch. After admiring the view from the water's edge return to the track, going left to gate of reserve.

▶ Enter reserve at left-hand gate (carefully closing it behind you). Keep to the path through oak woodland running parallel to Loch side

Gartocharn & the banks of Loch Lomond

2 Given clear weather, this south bank offers fine views up the loch. Inchcailloch lies next to Balmaha with Clairinsh in front of it, though Aber Isle is the nearest small islet. Moving west, Torrinch and Creinch line up along the Highland Boundary Fault, with a confusion of islands beyond.

3 This reserve is important as it represents what was once a much more extensive habitat in Scotland. Most marshes like the one lying further east as well as the oak-dominant woodland have now been lost in the lowlands, because of the needs of agriculture.

4 Visitors in May will enjoy a sheet of bluebells, flowering before the dense oak canopy begins to cut down the sunlight.

J Go through final gate at far end of wood leading to open field and Net Bay is ahead and to the left.

K At Net Bay Information board, take the gate to the right, climb through field keeping fence on the left, cross an old wall/hedge and Endrick Viewpoint information board is straight ahead. Retrace your steps all the way back to the post box at the junction at **F**.

5 In autumn and winter Endrick Viewpoint is a good place to see migrating birds and wintering wildfowl.

L At post box turn right and follow road on.

M Turn left at main road, left again opposite House of Darrach and so return to your starting point.

Loch Lomond

> 66 A short walk along a country road, through woodland to climb a small hill which offers magnificent views down Loch Lomond 99

Though Duncryne Hill is one of the shortest walks in the book it also offers one of the best views! Locally the hill is known as the Dumpling, at only 470ft (142m) it offers fantastic views. Duncryne Hill is an extinct volcano. It is first cousin to Dumbarton Rock, Dumgoyne and a number of other volcanic vents, that is, the inner core of a volcano, a whole series of which were responsible for the ancient Clyde Plateau lavas from which the Kilpatricks and Campsies (seen prominently from the top) are formed. Duncryne itself pokes through the Old Red Sandstone; fertile fields surround it, in spite of its position on the Highland edge. Its little dome is unmistakable, from whichever compass point you approach Gartocharn.

Duncryne Hill

Loch Lomond from Duncryne

Plan your walk

Crianlarich Lochearnhead

Callander

Aberfoyle

Stirling

Helensburgh Cumbernauld
Greenock Kirkintilloch

Paisley Glasgow

Motherwell

DISTANCE: 2 miles
(3.5km)

TIME: 1 hour

START/END: NS428863

TERRAIN: Easy

MAPS:
OS Explorer 347;
OS Landranger 56

Route instructions

A Gartocharn is on the A811 south of Loch Lomond. Park sensibly in the village; there is some parking near the church, reached by turning left (if coming from Balloch) opposite the House of Darrach and following the road round to the right. This is the same parking place as used for Gartocharn and Loch Lomond (Walk 17). Go back to the main road, turn left, cross over and take first right, up Duncryne Road, just past the House of Darrach. Go up this quiet country road for about half a mile and look for a layby, left, at the very end of the woodland also on the left. Alternatively, if time is short, drive here and make this your starting point.

B Go through the kissing gate and follow the path through woodland straight ahead. This section is very muddy in wet weather.

C Go through the kissing gate at wood edge, then follow the enclosed path across field to another kissing gate.

D Turn right and follow path to the top.

1 The view is quite unexpected and out of all proportion to the 470ft (142m) height. Nothing intrudes in the uninterrupted vista over the Highland Boundary Fault and into the high hills beyond. Between the Ochils in the east and the Clyde westward, the

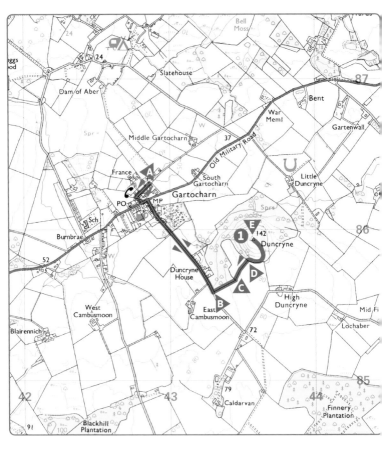

Duncryne Hill

Duncryne Hill

view encompasses the Perthshire Hills such as Ben More and Stob Binnein, round to the prominent Ben Lomond, Ben Vorlich (next left) and on to The Cobbler, and the Cowal Hills further west. But it is the loch and its islands that are most striking. Sea shells have been found in the terminal moraines, the materials dumped by glaciers, at the south end of the loch. This suggests that before the last Ice Age, the sea intruded up the Vale of Leven, seen conspicuously left. The last advance of the glaciers caused a wide dam of deposited material to form after they finally melted and withdrew. Only 27ft (8m) above sea level, Loch Lomond thus nearly became a sea loch like nearby Loch Long, a long fjord pointing far into the hills.

▶ Retrace your steps to the village.

> **❝** From the walk there are tremendous views of Loch Lomond with the mountains of the Highlands in the distance **❞**

The Whangie has been well-known to generations of Glasgow rock climbers. This strange geological phenomenon offers a wide variety of short but interesting pitches. For the walker it has scenic attractions, too, and is ideal for a short afternoon or evening's walk, enjoying views of Loch Lomond from these northern slopes of the Kilpatrick Hills. As for the geological reason for this peculiar, slightly eerie, even claustrophobic cleft, one explanation is an earthquake. There is a second explanation for the geological peculiarities of The Whangie. The Devil was in such a state of anticipation as he flew to a witches' meeting somewhere in the north, that he lashed his tail and carved off the rock slice through which the path now goes. It might even explain the odd atmosphere that surrounds the place, though given a fine evening you might not notice it. Concentrate instead on the larks, the curlews and the Queen's View from the car park.

The Whangie

Triangulation Point at the summit of Auchineden Hill

Route instructions

A The walk starts from a well-marked parking place and large car park about 7 miles (11.2km) north of Bearsden, Glasgow, on the A809 to Drymen. Alternatively, if travelling from Drymen, look for the site about 6 miles (9.6km) to the south, on the right.

B The path is unmistakable: over the stile in the wall, along the railway sleepers through the bog and uphill to the felled forestry on the skyline.

1 Note the hump of Dumgoyne, eastwards on the edge of the Campsie Fells.

C With most of the uphill section over, you reach a ladder stile; go over it. From

here a number of paths diverge, take one that bears left and climbs the hill above the line of crags. In unkind weather, however, it is easier to take the path that runs along the foot of these rocks. Do not lose height.

2 The view from the path, hemmed in between the fence below and the crags on your left, improves as you make your way towards The Whangie, as yet unseen. This is skylark country. Note the other little hump of Duncryne Hill, beyond the Stockie Muir, the moorland straight ahead, but in front of Loch Lomond to the north-west.

D Check that you are on a path which rises above a

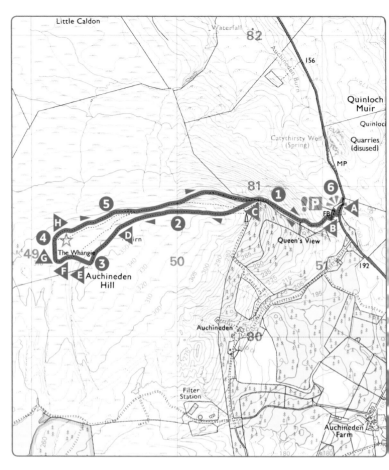

second line of rocks which start below you, right. As you near the top, a few paths come in to join from your left. Continue to triangulation point on Auchineden Hill.

3 Considering the nearness of the city of Glasgow, from the triangulation point there is a wide prospect over wild moorland, with Dumbarton Muir and the Kilpatricks to west and south.

E A number of trails wonder away from the triangulation point. Take the path that heads towards the left of Loch Lomond in the distance (westerly direction). If you go straight ahead, towards two reservoirs, then you will overshoot The Whangie and have to descend a steep west-facing section after only a few minutes, then divert sharp right along a faint path.

The Whangie

F You should find falling ground on both sides. Look for crags starting again on your right. This is the 'back door' of the Whangie.

G You enter by an unpromising-looking path which seems to disappear into the rock face.

4 You are now inside The Whangie with vertical rock walls rising on both sides. There is a gap that gives a fine view north-west to Loch Lomond.

H As you re-emerge, take the lowest path that you can find, going right and back along the face of the hill, retracing your footsteps to the ladder stile and down to the car park.

5 The small birds that show grey, buff, a black eye-stripe and a conspicuous white rump are wheatears, common in summer along this section. The bird's name is derived from Anglo-Saxon and literally means 'white-arse'.

6 For full details of the range of hills visible, check the excellent viewpoint indicator in the car-park.

View to Loch Lomond

> **“** Following the West Highland Way from Inverarnan this walk rewards you with splendid views down Loch Lomond **”**

A walk that takes advantage of an attractive part of the West Highland Way to gain a wonderful end-on view of Loch Lomond. It lies near ancient ways through the hills, used by cattle-drovers before the coming of the railways ended their trade. The area once supplied timber for iron smelting; the old Caledonian pine forest reached one of its most southerly limits in nearby Glen Falloch. Later, after the tourists arrived, the river that runs parallel to the walk described here was canalised between the end of Loch Lomond and the Drovers Inn. Steamers connected with stagecoaches at the hotel, which is also your starting point.

Inverarnan – Loch Lomond views

Drovers Inn, Inverarnan

Plan your walk

DISTANCE: 4½ miles (7.5km)

TIME: 2¼ hours

START/END: NN318184

TERRAIN: Moderate

MAPS:
OS Explorer 364;
OS Landranger 50 & 56

Route instructions

A The Drovers Inn has welcomed generations of walkers and climbers and is on the right as you go north, on the A82 beyond where Loch Lomond ends and Glen Falloch begins. Park in the car park. Turn right from the car park.

B Walk a few hundred yards along the footpath by the roadside, as far as the first bridge over the River Falloch. Turn right, cross the bridge and go right through a gate which is marked by West Highland Way indicators.

C Continue along the pleasant riverbank until the path meets the Ben Glas Burn (which has a fine waterfall much higher up the hillside, seen from the Drovers Inn). Then turn upstream and through a gate.

D Turn right and cross the footbridge, built by the Royal Engineers. Follow the path south until it almost rejoins the River Falloch.

1 If walking this route (and most other walks in this book) in moist weather in springtime, there may be a pleasing scent in the greenest of woodland, which does not come from any blossom. This is the scent given off by new birch leaves. You may notice it now as the path climbs into the birches.

walk 20 Inverarnan – Loch Lomond views **93**

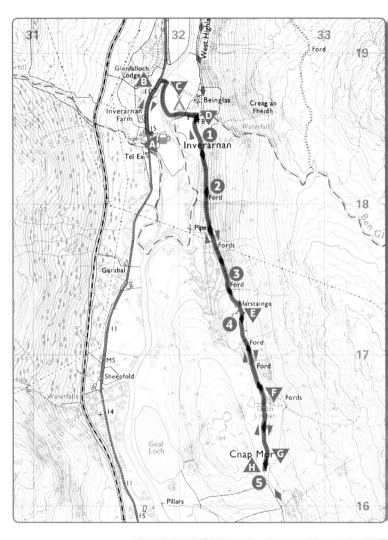

2 High above and out of sight, left, is the old drovers' route down to Glen Gyle from Glen Falloch. Rob Roy would have known it well.

3 In the wetter patches, butterwort, an insectivorous plant (like sundew) may be found. It looks like a little fleshy green starfish.

E Go through the ruined walls of the hamlet of Blarstainge, evidence that this deserted east

Inverarnan – Loch Lomond views

side of Glen Falloch once supported a much higher population.

4 From the hamlet, looking northwards up Glen Falloch, Ben Lui and Ben Oss are conspicuous, as is the nearer Ben Vorlich, southwards and on the other side of Loch Lomond.

F As you approach the Dubh Lochan, the 'little black loch' on your right, be careful, especially in wet weather there are several stretches where slippery railway sleepers form the path bed.

G To gain better views across Loch Lomond briefly leave the West Highland Way. Where the West Highland Way begins to drop down hill turn right on a faint path, follow this to the knoll top.

5 From the top, a magnificent view of Loch Lomond, lying in its narrow glacial trough, open out. Island I Vow is conspicuous.

H You may wish to make this a longer expedition by continuing down, eventually to reach the oak woods by the loch itself. There are also views across to Ardlui. Otherwise, retrace your steps back to Inverarnan.

View towards Inverarnan across Cnap Mor

Photo credits

All photographs © HarperCollins Publishers Ltd,
photographer Angela Mudge, with the exception of: